kids draw

ANIME

CHRISTOPHER HART

WATSON-GUPTILL PUBLICATIONS/
NEW YORK

Dedicated to anyone who has ever been told
that he or she watches too many cartoons.

Senior Editor: Julie Mazur
Designer: Bob Fillie, Graphiti Design, Inc.
Production Manager: Hector Campbell
Text set in 12-pt Frutiger Roman

Drawings on pages 52–64 by Andy Kuhn;
drawings on pages 15–16, 26–27,
and 42–45 by Svetlana Chmakova.
All other drawings by Christopher Hart.

Cover art by Christopher Hart

First published in 2002 by
Watson-Guptill Publications, an imprint of the Crown Publishing Group,
a division of Random House Inc., New York
www.crownpublishing.com
www.watsonguptill.com

Library of Congress Cataloging-in-Publication Data
Hart, Christopher.
    Kids draw anime / Christopher Hart.
            p. cm.
Includes index.
Summary: Provides step-by-step instructions for drawing a variety
of human, animal, and other figures in the style of Japanese anime,
covering general tips, details of specific features, and how to show action.
    ISBN 0-8230-2690-6
1. Comic books, strips, etc.—Japan—Technique—Juvenile literature.
2. Drawing—Technique—Juvenile literature. [1. Cartoons and comics.
2. Drawing—Technique.] I. Title: Anime. II. Title.

    NC1764.5.J3 H3698 2002
    741.5—dc21

                                    2002006799

CONTENTS

INTRODUCTION

Did you know that *anime* is the Japanese word for "animation"? Anime is Japanese cartoons. Anime started in—you guessed it—Japan, but is now hugely popular all over the world. Pokémon, Dragon Ball Z, Digimon, Sailor Moon—these are all examples of anime.

If you've ever wondered how to draw cool anime characters yourself, this is the book for you! You'll learn to draw their "shiny" eyes, tiny noses, and crazy expressions. You'll create all kinds of anime-style characters, from evil scientists to cute girls and boys, fantasy characters, action heroes, animals, and more.

Along the way, you'll pick up important drawing skills, like how to get proportions right, drawing the head at different angles, using *foreshortening,* and more.

Hey, there's no time to waste. The earth has to be defended against invading aliens and we have to draw anime heroes to lead the battle! Ready for action?

ANIME

Let's start with the very basics, like drawing anime eyes, heads, bodies, and those tricky hands and feet.

The drawings in this book go step by step. Each one starts with an easy form and then builds on it.

   Here's an example. This is an anime-style head at a 3/4 view. A 3/4 view means the character isn't looking straight to the front or straight to the side, but somewhere in between.

Anime characters are famous for their huge eyes. These eyes are drawn differently if the character is facing the front, or the side. Let's find out how.

WRONG

FRONT VIEW
From the front, the eye is almond shaped.

SIDE VIEW
From the side, the eye is wide at the front, but narrows to a point in the back.

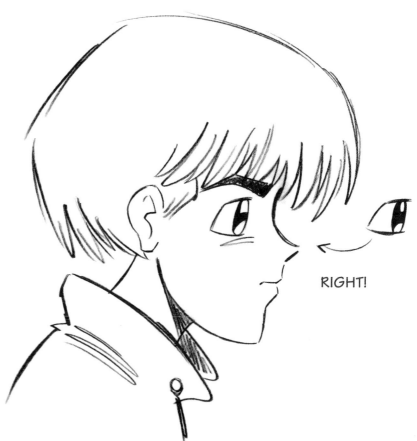

RIGHT!

7

Adding the Shine

Anime artists add "shine" to make the eyes sparkle. The shine is light reflecting off the dark parts of the eye.

Sometimes anime artists use two, three, or more shines to give the eyes extra "oomph." Try the eyes here, then make up your own!

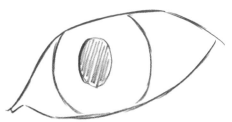

Start with a basic eye.

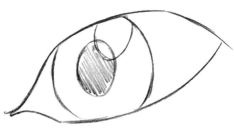

Add the shine so it overlaps both the iris and the pupil.

Add a shadow around the shine. Make sure it doesn't go into the "white" of the eye.

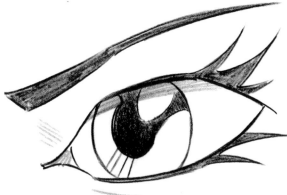

Add eyelashes, a tear duct, and some lines to show the iris. Done!

SINGLE SHINE
Here's your basic shine. It usually appears on the top half of the eye.

TWO SHINES
If you add another shine, make the top shine a little smaller so there's still plenty of black.

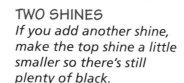

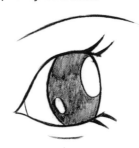

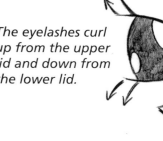

The eyelashes curl up from the upper lid and down from the lower lid.

The line of the nose curves around to become the eyebrow.

MANY SHINES
Here are two ways to show lots of shines. The top eye has only a huge pupil. The bottom eye shows a pupil with an iris around it.

CARTOONY
Notice how "tall" these eyes are. This style is usually used for young anime characters.

WHY SO MANY SHINES?
Most light comes from above, such as from ceiling lights or sunshine. This light shines down and reflects off the top half of the eye—so we put a shine there. But the light also travels to the ground, then bounces up and reflects off the *bottom* of the eye. This is called *reflected light*. Reflected light creates a second shine.

Why is the bottom shine smaller? Reflected light travels farther, so it's not as strong as overhead light. The shine isn't as strong either.

Anime Noses

There are many types of anime-style noses, but all are small and delicate. Some are no more than a shadow. Which nose below do you like best? Part of being an artist is making choices.

Here's the most common kind of anime nose.

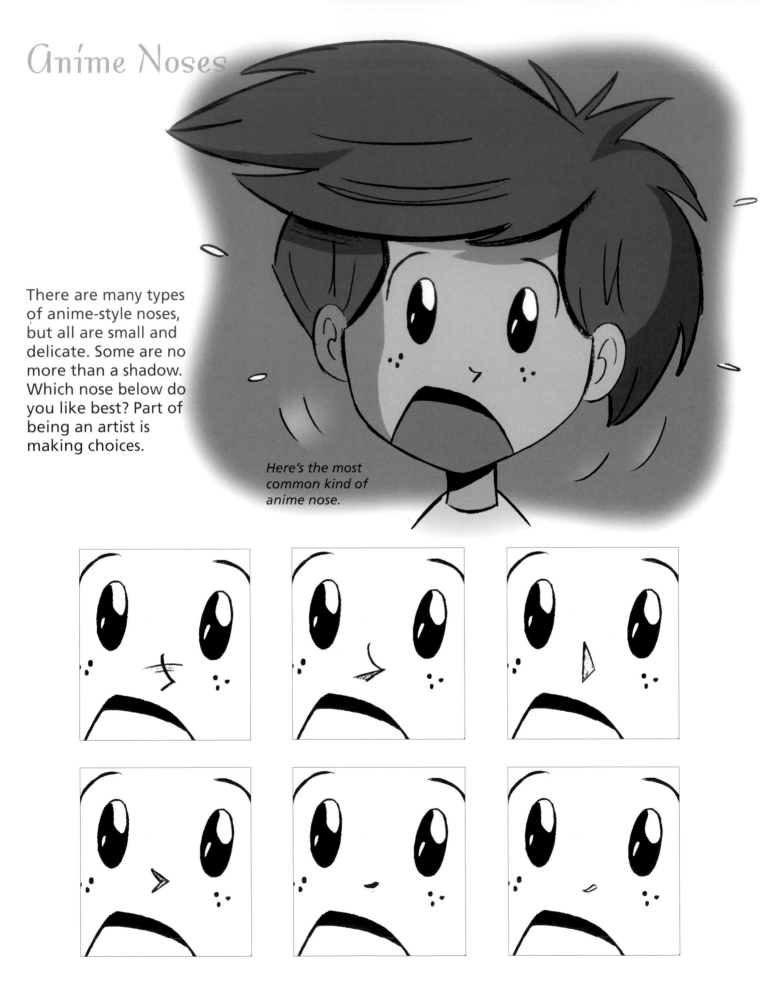

Most anime faces share the same basic proportions. The eyes are far apart, the nose is close to the mouth, and the chin is long. Here are some tips for checking the proportions in your drawings.

Notice how wide apart her eyes are. The space between her nose and mouth is short. There is more space between her mouth and chin.

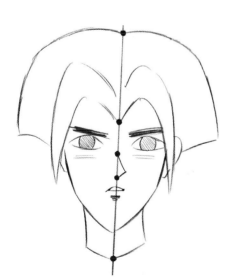

THE CENTERLINE
To make sure the left and right sides are the same, draw a light line down the center of the face. You can also use this line to place parts of the face: the part in the middle of the hair, the bridge of the nose, the bottom of the nose, and the pit of the neck.

THE EYE LINE
To see if the eyes are even, draw light lines across the tops and bottoms of both eyes. The lines should go straight across.

LINES FOR THE EARS, NOSE, AND EYEBROWS
To check the ears, draw a light line across the tops and bottoms of both ears. The eyebrows should sit on the top line. The bottom of the nose should sit on the lower line.

Let's start with the front view of a young evil genius.

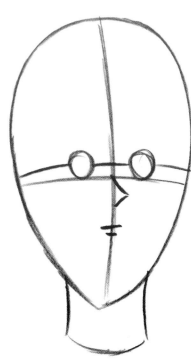

The head is an oval, or egg shape. The centerline divides the head in half from top to bottom. The eye line divides it in half from side to side.

Put the eyes on the eye line. I'm giving this character glasses, which rest on the eye line. Draw a tiny nose and a small mouth.

Add the hair above the head. Add the ears so their tops fall near the eye line. Try not to draw the eyebrows super straight.

Give him a choppy hairstyle. Add shoulders.

Use your eraser to make shines in his hair. Add small shadows on the side of his nose, under his bottom lip, and under his chin. Finished!

...and Side View

For a side view, it's important to get the outline of the face done well. The features are easier to draw because there's only one of each, so you don't have to worry if they're even!

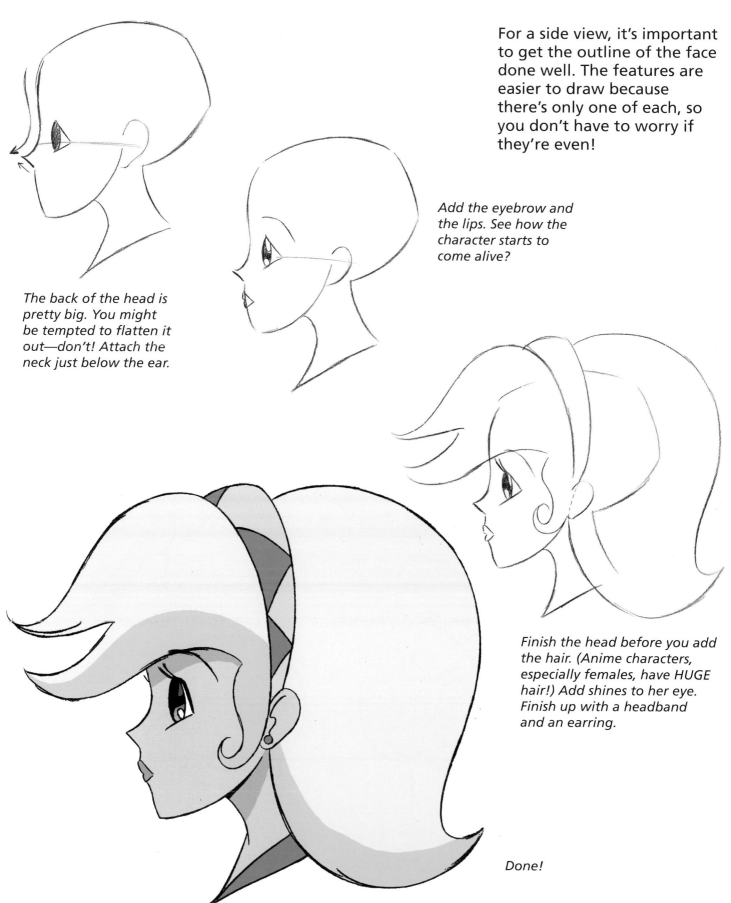

The back of the head is pretty big. You might be tempted to flatten it out—don't! Attach the neck just below the ear.

Add the eyebrow and the lips. See how the character starts to come alive?

Finish the head before you add the hair. (Anime characters, especially females, have HUGE hair!) Add shines to her eye. Finish up with a headband and an earring.

Done!

Tilting the Head

In real life, we hardly ever stand in a perfect front or side view. Usually, our heads are tilted one way or another. Think of the head as a block of wood. As you turn the block, different sides become visible.

Practice some of the heads shown here. Then change the faces to make up your own characters.

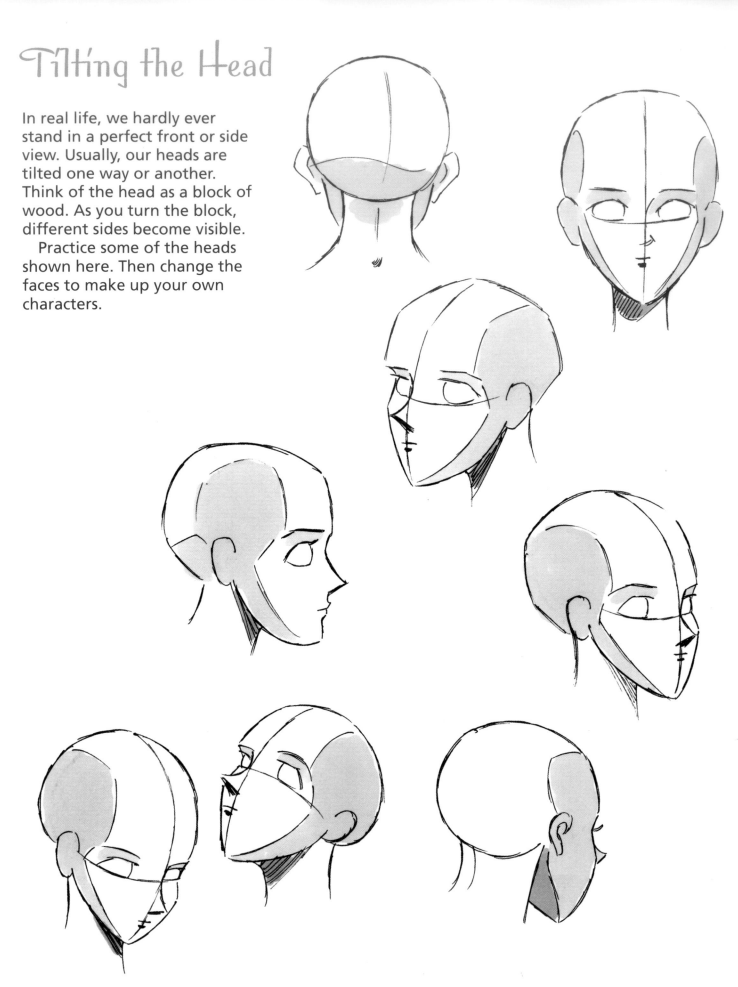

Adding Expressions

Anime boys and girls are full of energy and their emotions bubble over! You can show this with special effects, such as blush marks, stars, hearts, tears, speed lines, and sound effects. Even the background can change color to show a character's emotions.

ANNOYED

EMBARRASSED

EXCITED

SUSPICIOUS

SKRITCH

AGGRESSIVE

AMBITIOUS

INFATUATED

FUNNY

SAD

MAD

SPIRITED

HAPPY

If you're drawing someone who's mad, make her really, really mad. If you're drawing someone sad, add big eyes and tears. In cartooning, always make the emotions larger than life.

INTENSE

TRIUMPHANT

SURPRISED

CURIOUS

SSIZZLE

VENGEFUL

HUMILIATED

ZZZZZZ

SLEEPY

WORRIED

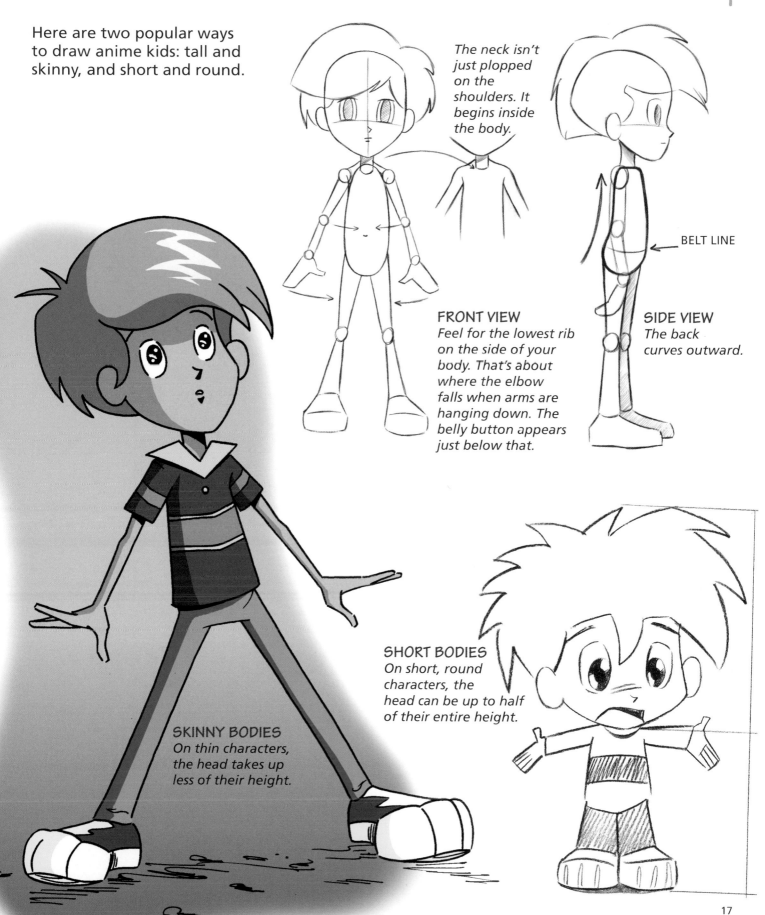

Here are two popular ways to draw anime kids: tall and skinny, and short and round.

The neck isn't just plopped on the shoulders. It begins inside the body.

FRONT VIEW
Feel for the lowest rib on the side of your body. That's about where the elbow falls when arms are hanging down. The belly button appears just below that.

BELT LINE

SIDE VIEW
The back curves outward.

SKINNY BODIES
On thin characters, the head takes up less of their height.

SHORT BODIES
On short, round characters, the head can be up to half of their entire height.

17

Look at how the body gets put together. Then follow the drawings to build a body yourself.

When you draw clothes, show a small fold where the shoulder meets the arm. This fold goes in toward the chest (short arrows).

The shoulders slope down from the neck (long arrows).

The hips curve out. They are wider than the waist.

From the front, feet look thinnest at the ankle. They widen out at the toes.

Here are more tips for drawing different anime bodies.

CUTE BODIES

Characters with big heads and short, round bodies are called *chibi*-style. (*Chibi* means "little" in Japanese.) The head takes up almost half of the entire height. The tummy is pushed out, and the arms and legs are short.

SKINNY BODIES

Thin characters have long arms and legs. Their heads take up less of their height than with *chibi*-style characters.

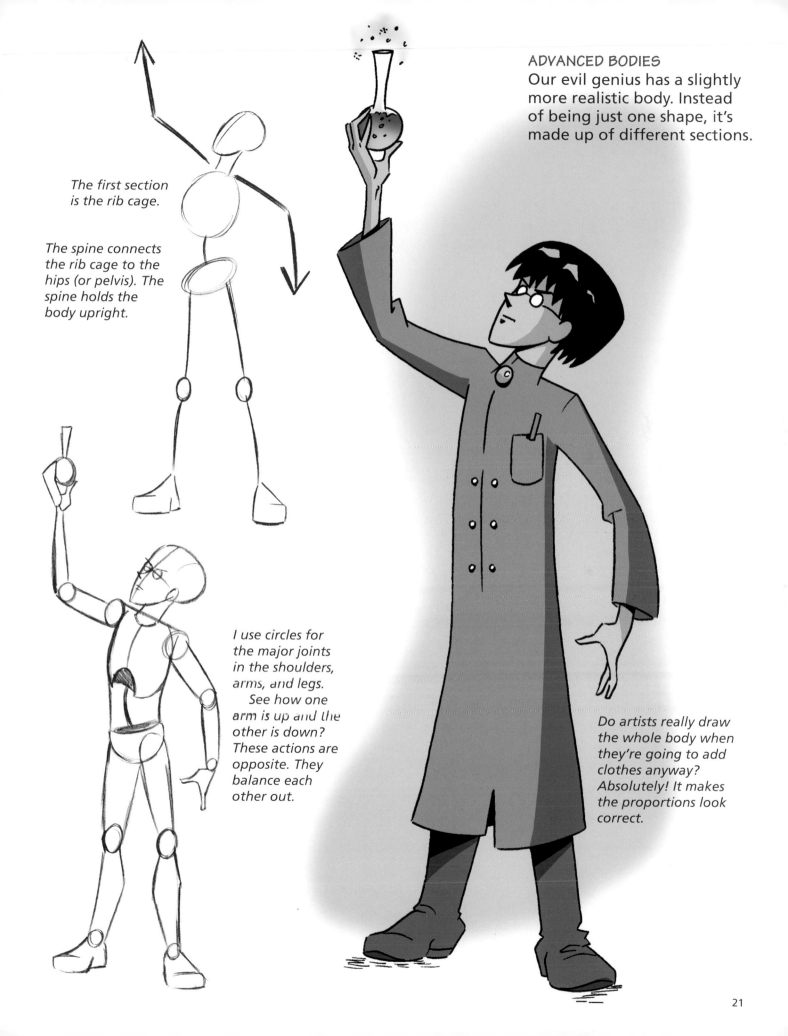

The first section is the rib cage.

The spine connects the rib cage to the hips (or pelvis). The spine holds the body upright.

I use circles for the major joints in the shoulders, arms, and legs.
    See how one arm is up and the other is down? These actions are opposite. They balance each other out.

ADVANCED BODIES
Our evil genius has a slightly more realistic body. Instead of being just one shape, it's made up of different sections.

Do artists really draw the whole body when they're going to add clothes anyway? Absolutely! It makes the proportions look correct.

Easy Hands

Hands are easy to draw when you do them step by step.

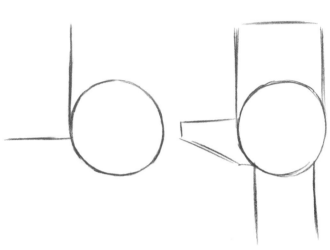
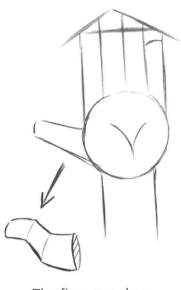
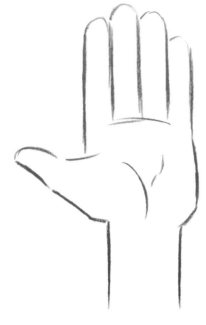

PALM-UP VIEW

Draw the main "body" of the hand (the palm) first. Add two lines for the first finger and thumb.

Figure out where the fingers go. Add the thumb and wrist. The thumb gets thicker near the wrist.

The fingers make a "pyramid." The middle finger is the tallest. Draw each finger separately.

You've got it! Notice the curves of the thumb. The thumb really has three sections.

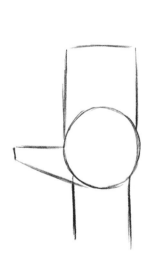
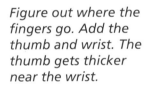
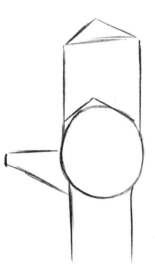
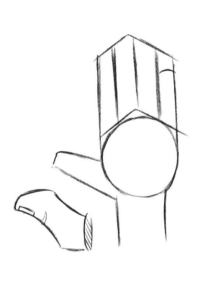

BACK OF HAND VIEW

Start with this shape, which shows where all the parts will go.

Draw the fingers as a pyramid. Make the knuckles a pyramid, too. The middle knuckle is the tallest.

Draw each separate finger and the curve of the thumb.

Done!

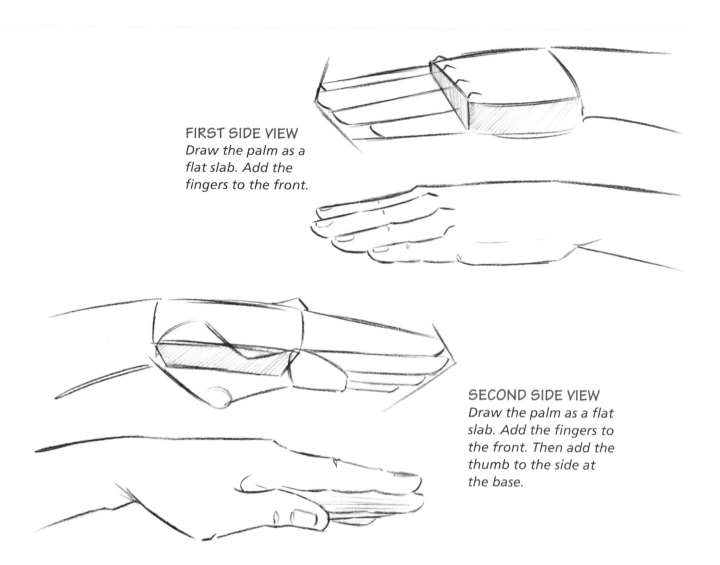

FIRST SIDE VIEW
Draw the palm as a flat slab. Add the fingers to the front.

SECOND SIDE VIEW
Draw the palm as a flat slab. Add the fingers to the front. Then add the thumb to the side at the base.

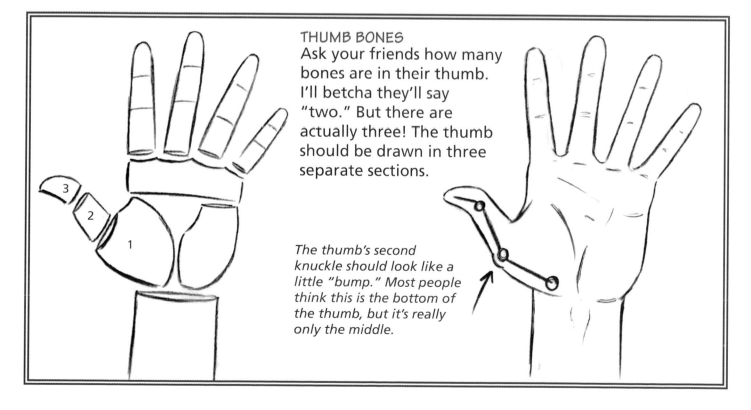

THUMB BONES
Ask your friends how many bones are in their thumb. I'll betcha they'll say "two." But there are actually three! The thumb should be drawn in three separate sections.

The thumb's second knuckle should look like a little "bump." Most people think this is the bottom of the thumb, but it's really only the middle.

Advanced Hands

Here are some cool hand poses to practice.

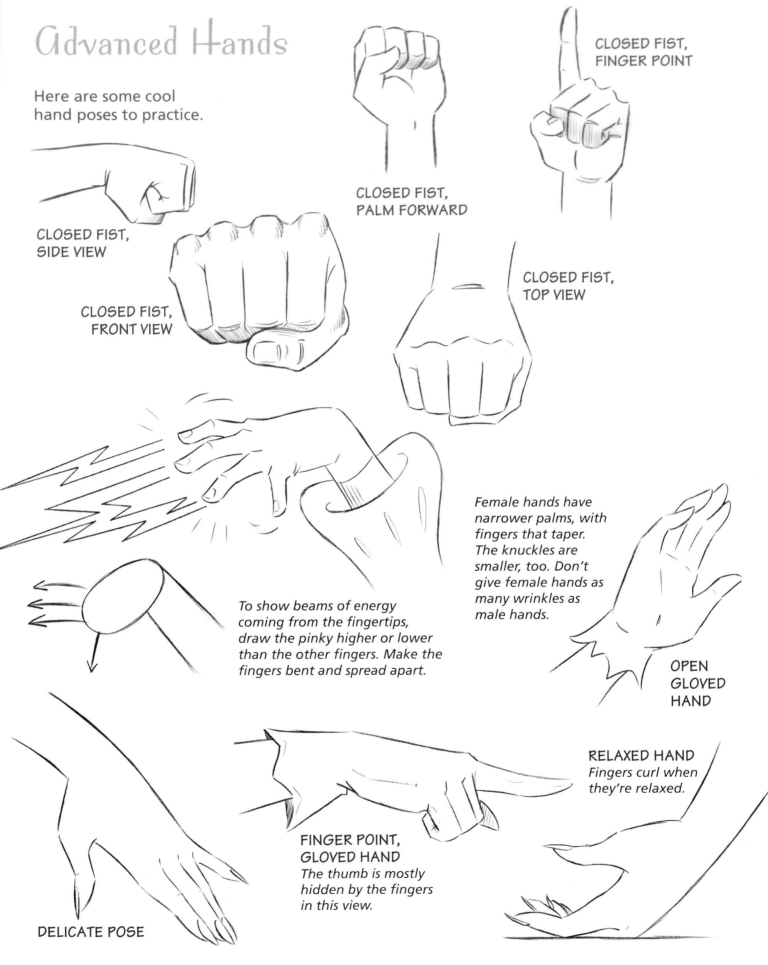

CLOSED FIST, PALM FORWARD

CLOSED FIST, FINGER POINT

CLOSED FIST, SIDE VIEW

CLOSED FIST, FRONT VIEW

CLOSED FIST, TOP VIEW

To show beams of energy coming from the fingertips, draw the pinky higher or lower than the other fingers. Make the fingers bent and spread apart.

Female hands have narrower palms, with fingers that taper. The knuckles are smaller, too. Don't give female hands as many wrinkles as male hands.

OPEN GLOVED HAND

RELAXED HAND
Fingers curl when they're relaxed.

FINGER POINT, GLOVED HAND
The thumb is mostly hidden by the fingers in this view.

DELICATE POSE

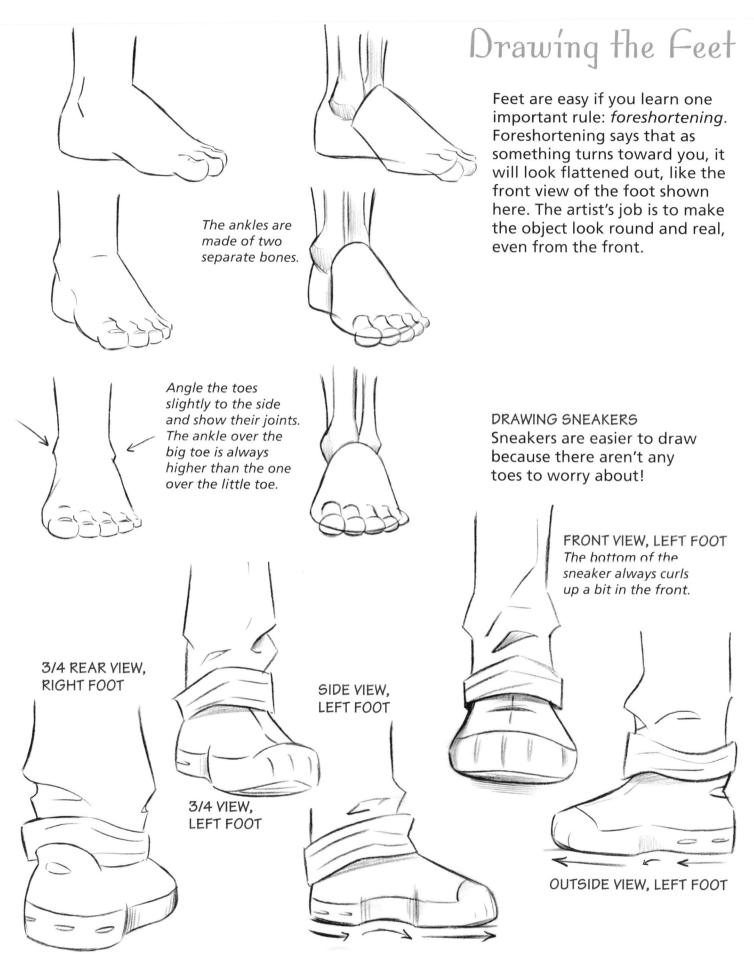

Drawing the Feet

Feet are easy if you learn one important rule: *foreshortening*. Foreshortening says that as something turns toward you, it will look flattened out, like the front view of the foot shown here. The artist's job is to make the object look round and real, even from the front.

The ankles are made of two separate bones.

Angle the toes slightly to the side and show their joints. The ankle over the big toe is always higher than the one over the little toe.

DRAWING SNEAKERS
Sneakers are easier to draw because there aren't any toes to worry about!

FRONT VIEW, LEFT FOOT
The bottom of the sneaker always curls up a bit in the front.

3/4 REAR VIEW, RIGHT FOOT

3/4 VIEW, LEFT FOOT

SIDE VIEW, LEFT FOOT

OUTSIDE VIEW, LEFT FOOT

Using the "Action Line"

Artists create exciting poses by using the *action line.* This is a guideline that sets the basic pose. It's like a "check" to make sure the pose isn't straight and boring. The action line usually follows the flow of the character's spine.

When you draw your own characters, start with a very light action line. Then build the pose around the line. Erase the action line when you're done.

EASY ANIME CHARACTERS

O kay, you've got the basics. Now let's use what you've learned to draw some fun anime characters!

What Makes a "Bad Guy" (or "Girl"!)?

Admit it, bad guys and gals are fun to draw. But what is it that makes them look "bad?" Here are some tips for creating that cool anime badness.

GOOD GUY

- FULLER FACE
- BIG, OPEN EYES
- SMALL NOSE
- BUSHY HAIR
- BOLD EYEBROWS
- CLEAN, YOUNG APPEARANCE

BAD GUY

- NARROW FACE
- BEADY, NARROW EYES
- POINTY NOSE
- LONG, STRINGY HAIR
- FACE PARTLY IN SHADOW
- OLDER APPEARANCE
- GRUBBY LOOK (UNSHAVEN)

Want an easy way to draw a bad guy? Start with an evil smile and add angry eyebrows. Voilà! Sharp cheekbones also help. So do tiny little pupils, bony fingers, yucky fingernails, and crazy hair. This evil guy also has bad skin, plenty of wrinkles, and a thin face.

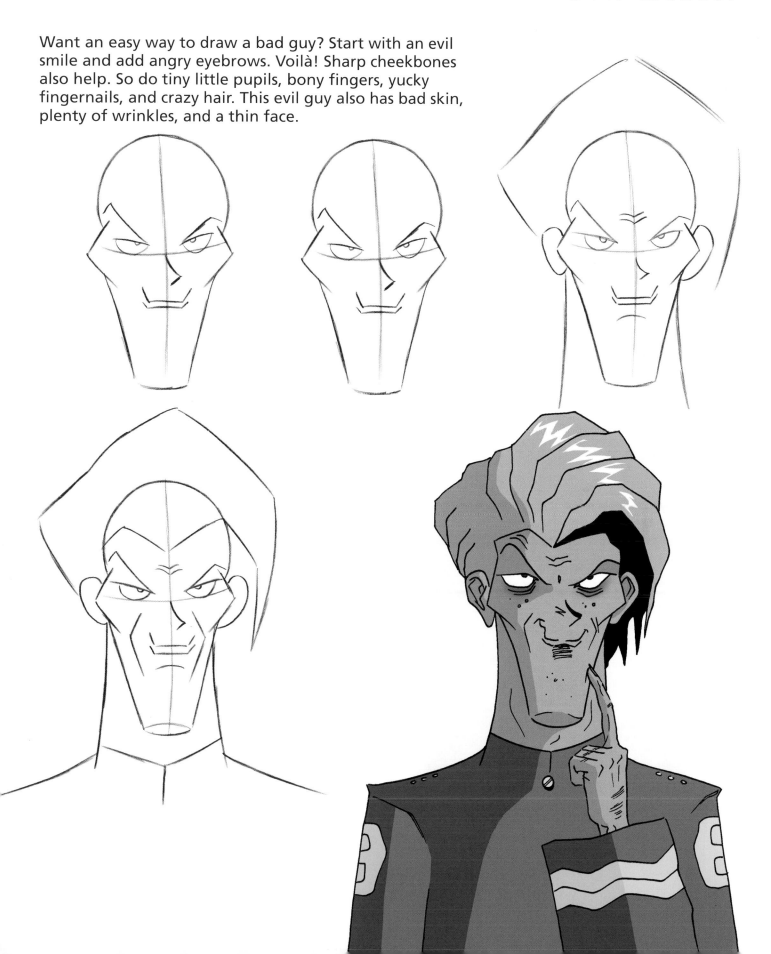

Cool Bad Guy

This teenage rebel rides a giant motorcycle—always a sign of badness. Other tip-offs are his facial stubble (good guys are clean-cut), his leather jacket, and his mean-looking attitude. He's out for number one: himself!

THE BACKGROUND

Draw the guy in the middle of the page

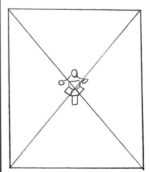

Draw an "x."

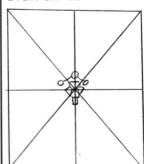

Draw a line down the center of the page and a second line across the middle of the page.

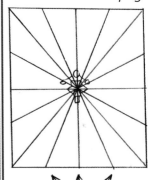

Add a line between every other line. Erase the bottom three lines to form the road.

Elfin Creatures

Enchanted forest creatures also dwell in anime's fantasy kingdom. Let your imagination take you deep into the forest, where tiny winged creatures use magic forces to defend themselves against evil.

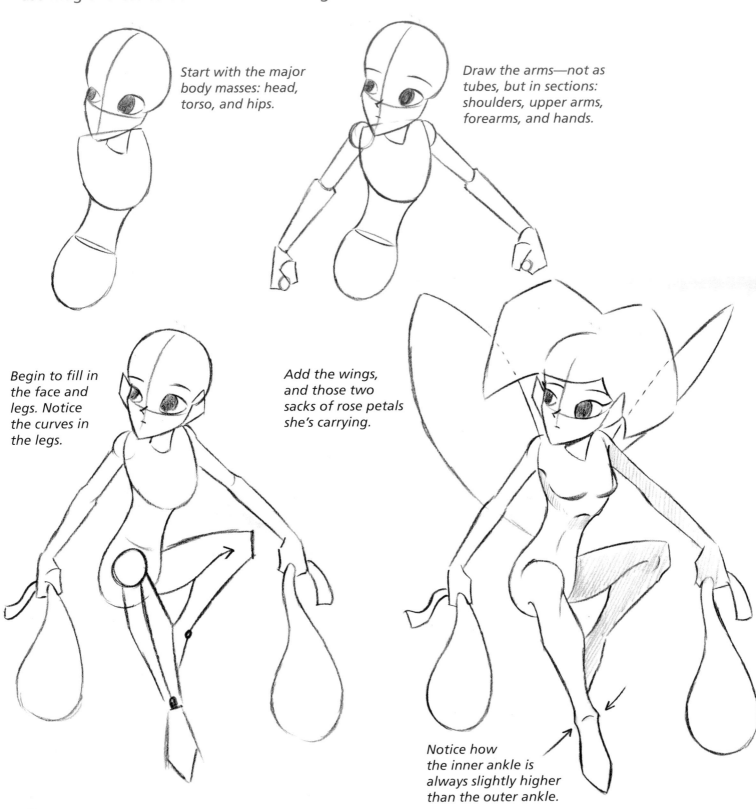

Start with the major body masses: head, torso, and hips.

Draw the arms—not as tubes, but in sections: shoulders, upper arms, forearms, and hands.

Begin to fill in the face and legs. Notice the curves in the legs.

Add the wings, and those two sacks of rose petals she's carrying.

Notice how the inner ankle is always slightly higher than the outer ankle.

Young Knight

Young knights (called *squires*) are popular in anime because they are such unlikely heroes.

A Boy & His Dragon

Tiny monsters are also popular in anime. Here, a squire has made friends with a miniature dragon. I've made the boy look wide-eyed with wonder by giving him tall eyes with lots of shines.

Space Command

Uh-oh, here comes an alien vessel! Is it friendly or evil? Even though this commander's cape covers much of his body, you should start by sketching his entire body first. Don't skip the early steps—they'll pay off later.

Anime Robots

Robots stand as tall as skyscrapers in anime cartoons. They have special weapons hidden all over their bodies.

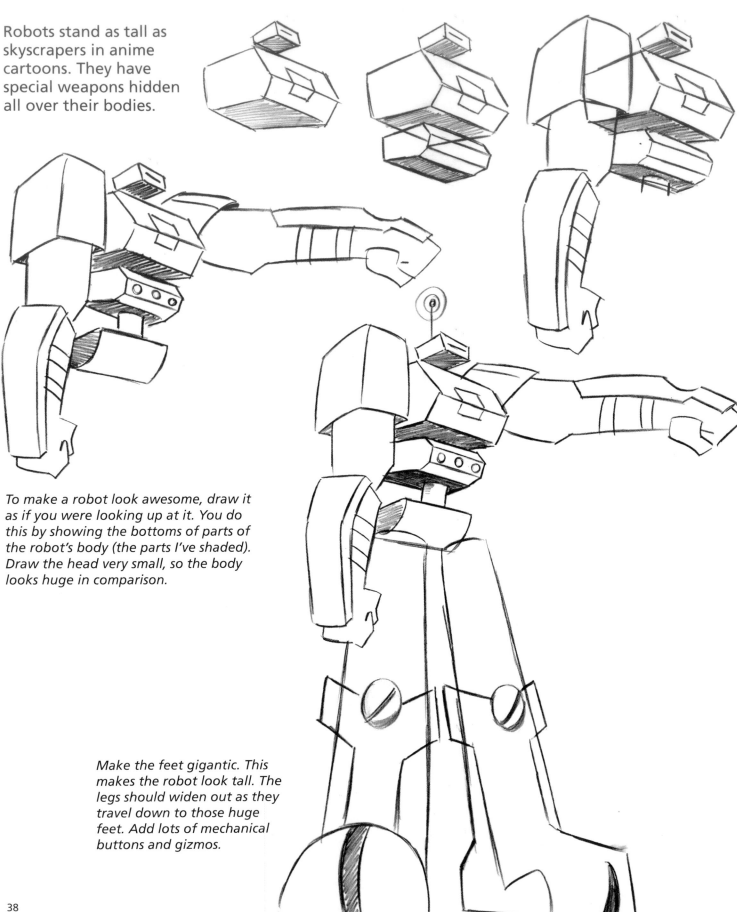

To make a robot look awesome, draw it as if you were looking up at it. You do this by showing the bottoms of parts of the robot's body (the parts I've shaded). Draw the head very small, so the body looks huge in comparison.

Make the feet gigantic. This makes the robot look tall. The legs should widen out as they travel down to those huge feet. Add lots of mechanical buttons and gizmos.

You can tell this robot is taking orders from far away because of the radio transmissions he's receiving on top of his head.

Turning Any Creature into a Robot

Any animal or vehicle can be made into a fierce robot. This one is based on a gorilla.

To make a robot out of an animal, just draw the animal's body in sections, like toys that snap together. Every part of the robot should be a separate section.

To make the robot look gigantic, put a normal person or animal in the picture to show the difference in size, like the boy shown here. Add futuristic doodads, like spikes, antennae, and knobs. Then set the robot loose and get out of the way!

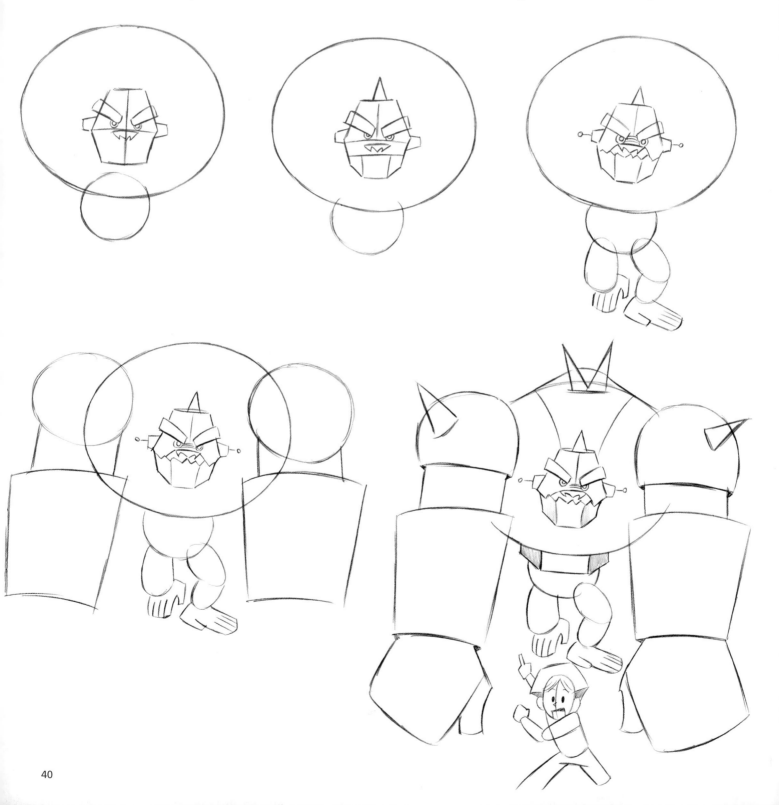

ANIME ANIMALS

Just like the humans, animals in anime have wide eyes and subtle faces. They're drawn sort of realistically, but with more expression and spirit than animals in real life.

Playful Cat

This little fur ball is finding all sorts of things to do while her owner is gone.

Monkey

The golden lion tamarin monkey has big eyes, a flowing mane, and a large, bushy tail. Looks like someone's campsite got raided by this hungry little fella!

Panda Bear

They're irresistible, they're chubby, and they're big! Like all bears, panda bears sit and stand in ways that almost look human.

The panda's body is made of two large ovals, or flattened circles.

How do pandas get so fat when they only eat bamboo?

Horse

Horses are huge, muscular animals. Their legs have no fur or fat covering them up, so you have to draw them just right.

This is a good pose to start with because the legs are spaced apart and easy to see. Follow each step, and you'll be drawing galloping anime horses in no time!

THE MARTIAL ARTS

The heroes and heroines of martial arts are very disciplined. They follow strict tradition and honor their masters, teachers, and emperor.

Martial Arts Master

Martial arts masters are very serious. They wear clothing that shows their rank, from beginner to expert. They usually rest in a seated, kneeling position, like the one shown here.

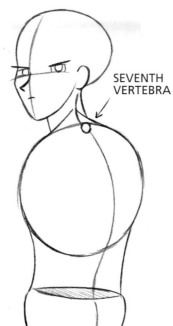

SEVENTH VERTEBRA

See that bone sticking out on the back of his neck? That's the seventh vertebra. You can feel it on the back of your own neck, too. It's the one that sticks out the most.

Once the basic form is in place, add the clothing. Notice how the belt pulls the clothing in tightly around the waist. The clothes puff out above and below it.

This is a "rough." It's ready to be cleaned up as a finished drawing.

Fearless Samurai

The samurai is legendary in anime and folklore. He was a noble warrior who protected the emperor.

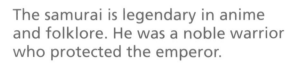

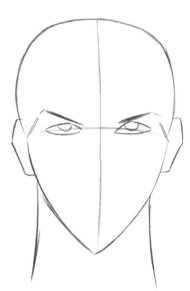

Start with an egg-shaped head. Add the guidelines. To make this warrior look deadly serious, bury half of his eyes under his top lids and draw him staring directly at you.

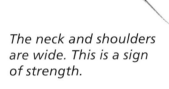

The neck and shoulders are wide. This is a sign of strength.

The outline of the muscles travels down the neck to where the collarbones meet.

You're done!

Martial Arts Grand Master

Old masters have amazing knowledge and mysterious skills. They can send an enemy flying with just a flick of the wrist. Next time, don't call him "grandpa"!

OLD VERSUS YOUNG CHARACTERS
Check out these tips for making a character look young or old.

YOUNG

NECK SHOWS

CHEST STICKS OUT

OLD

NO NECK

CHEST CURVES IN

The Famous Flying Side Kick

The flying side kick is done by kicking one leg straight out and tucking the other underneath. This character is wearing a kung-fu outfit. You can tell because the jacket is buttoned down the middle. Kung fu is a very old martial art from China.

The martial artist leans forward with her upper body. She puts all of her body force into the kick.

This "rough" is an example of how artists work in the early stages of a drawing. So don't think that your drawing has to be perfect from the start!

HEEL

KNIFE BLADE

There are two surfaces of the foot that can be used to strike during a side kick: the heel and the "knife blade."

Starbursts and speed lines give your drawing extra "flash"—like using an exclamation point at the end of a sentence!

Hi-YA!

Use starbursts at the point of impact.

Use speed lines to show motion along the way.

YA!

Teen Warrior

This drawing and the ones that follow show more advanced action figures. Start with looser, lighter lines. And don't be afraid to erase!

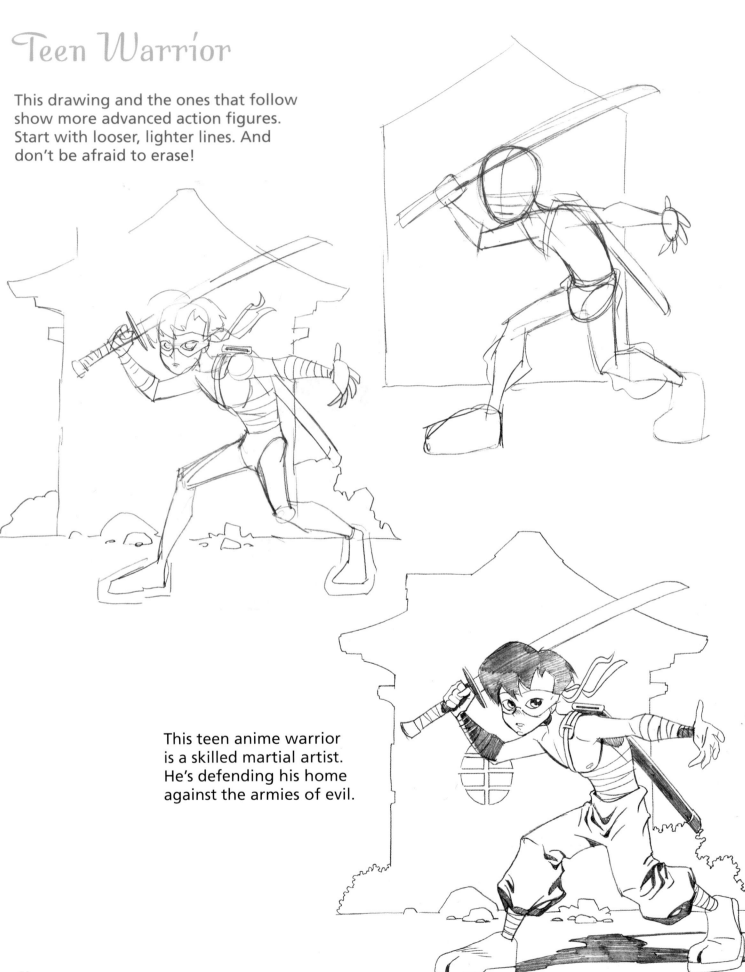

This teen anime warrior is a skilled martial artist. He's defending his home against the armies of evil.

AMAZING ACTION HEROES!

Roll up your sleeves, anime fans, because we're going full-speed ahead! With all you've learned so far, you're ready to tackle cutting-edge anime action!

Air Surfer

This bad boy uses a remote control attached to his arm to steer his flying surfboard.

Evil Lady Creature

This lady is evil through and through. First there's her hair, which hides part of her face (a sneaky look for bad guys and gals). She's also got dragon's wings, which you don't usually find on the girl next door.

Circles that overlap each other are signs of magic and sorcery. She has the power to create dark magic spells, and hypnotize people against their will.

Too Hot to Handle!

When this fiery lady is in danger, her body glows red hot and emits flames. Things around her burst into fire. If you plan to attack her, do it near a sprinkler system!

Super Strength

To show superhuman strength, show
your character with objects that look
too big for normal humans to handle.

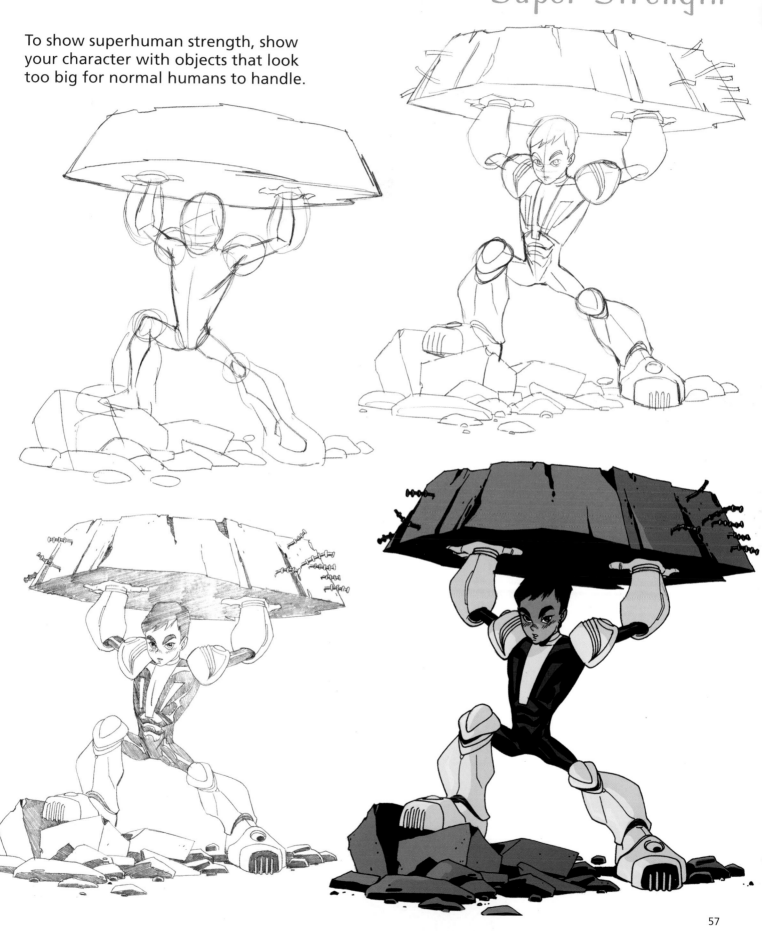

Tons of characters, with tons of special effects! Each character is showing off his or her amazing powers.

Giant Dinosaur Mutant

Anime dinosaurs are mean and hungry. And for some reason, they always think a big city would be a good place to get a snack.

Dinosaurs should tower over skyscrapers and even over the clouds. Their skin should look craggy and scaly. Plates on their backs create a dinosaur look. And notice the lines on this guy's belly, a clear mark of a lizard.

Monster Insect

If you thought that last creature couldn't get any uglier, meet his cousin. This cross between a huge iguana and a fly is about the most repulsive thing I've ever seen!

This guy has lots of wings, all of them different lengths. This makes him look more menacing than if there were only two wings of the same length, which is what you find on some drawings of fairies. His many arms are also creepy. Why? Because they remind us of insects.

Index

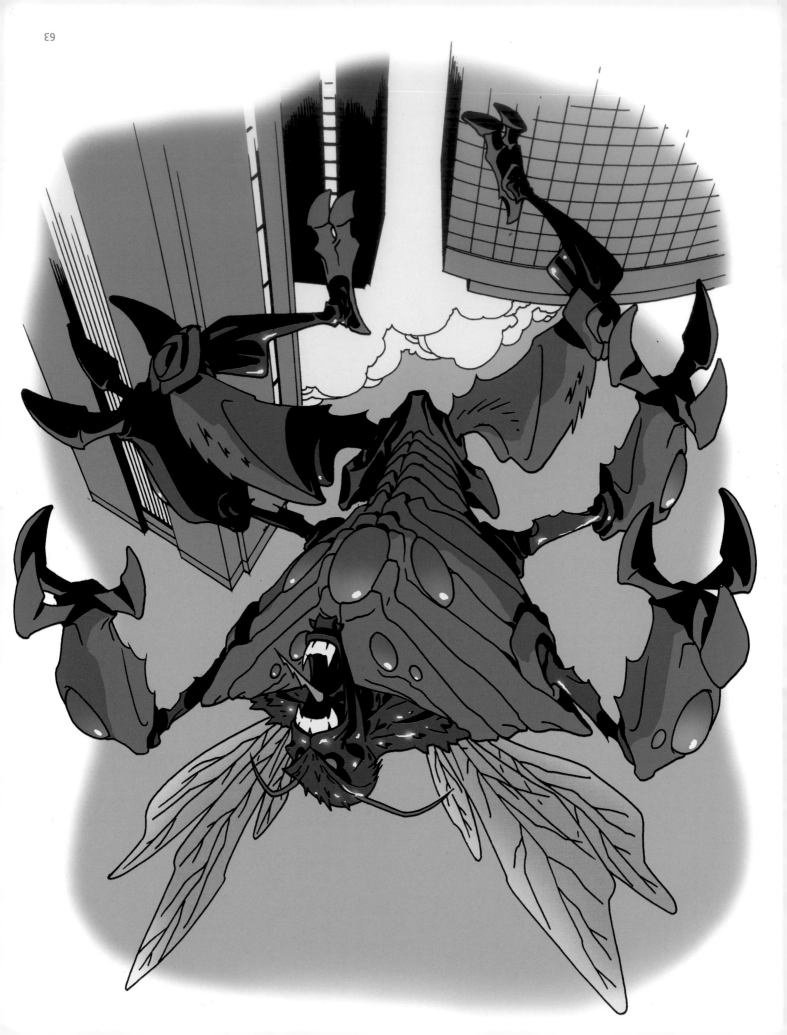